Georgia, My State
Rocks and Minerals

Rocks and Minerals
of the
Piedmont

by Samantha Stanford

STATE
STANDARDS
PUBLISHING ®

Your State • Your Standards • Your Grade Level

Dear Educators, Librarians and Parents . . .

Thank you for choosing the *"Georgia, My State"* Series! We have designed this series to support the Georgia Department of Education's Georgia Performance Standards for elementary level Georgia studies. Each book in the series has been written at appropriate grade level as measured by the ATOS Readability Formula for Books (Accelerated Reader), the Lexile Framework for Reading, and the Fountas & Pinnell Benchmark Assessment System for Guided Reading. Photographs and/or illustrations, captions, and other design elements have been included to provide supportive visual messaging to enhance text comprehension. Glossary and Word Index sections introduce key new words and help young readers develop skills in locating and combining information.

We wish you all success in using the *"Georgia, My State"* Series to meet your student or child's learning needs. For additional sources of information, see www.georgiaencyclopedia.org.

Jill Ward, President

Publisher
State Standards Publishing, LLC
1788 Quail Hollow
Hamilton, GA 31811
USA
1.866.740.3056
www.statestandardspublishing.com

Library of Congress Control Number: 2010933590

Printed in the United States of America, North Mankato, Minnesota, August 2010, 082010.

About the Author

Samantha Stanford graduated with honors from Columbus State University in Columbus, Georgia with a degree in geology. She is pursuing a Master of Science in geology at the University of North Carolina at Wilmington, with plans to earn a doctorate in paleontology. Her research has been published in the *New Mexico Museum of Natural History & Science Bulletins* and featured in *National Geographic Daily News*. She enjoys spending her free time collecting fossils with her husband, Chris, and their dogs, Maya and Caiman.

Table of Contents

The Rock Cycle

Cools and Lifts

Igneous Rock

Erosion

Magma

Sediment

Melting

Metamorphic Rock

Pressed Together Under Water

Heat and Pressure Underground

Sedimentary Rock

What are Rocks and Minerals?

Hi, I'm Bagster. Let's explore rocks and minerals in Georgia! A **mineral** is a natural material that is not alive like plants and animals. A **rock** is made of two or more minerals. Think of a rock as being like a cake. The flour, butter, and eggs in the cake would be minerals. The whole cake would be the rock. There are three kinds of rocks. **Igneous** rocks are made from hot liquid rock called **magma**. **Sedimentary** rocks are made from igneous rocks. Rain and wind break the rocks into tiny pieces called **sediment**. This process is called **erosion**. **Metamorphic** rocks form when igneous or sedimentary rocks are pushed underground and heat up. Rocks can change from one type to another and back again. This process is called the **rock cycle**.

Clay sometimes makes rivers look muddy.

Appalachian Plateau
Blue Ridge Mountains
Valley and Ridge
★ Atlanta
Piedmont
Coastal Plain

There are lots of rolling hills in the Piedmont.

The Piedmont Rolls!

Let's explore the Piedmont **geographic region**. A region is an area named for the way the land is formed. The Piedmont sits at the bottom of the Blue Ridge Mountains region. Piedmont means *foot of the mountains*. There are lots of rolling hills in the Piedmont. Georgia's state capital, Atlanta, is in the Piedmont region.

The soil in the Piedmont is mostly red clay. Clay soil is sticky and thick when wet and hard when dry. Piedmont clay has tiny bits of iron in it. Iron is a **metal**. Metal is a substance that conducts heat or electricity. Iron rusts. It turns things red. Clay in the Piedmont can stain your clothes and shoes. It can also make rivers look muddy.

Red Clay Soil

Granite Countertop

Mica

Quartz

Feldspar

Stone Mountain is the largest piece of granite you can see in the world!

Georgia's Granite

Stone Mountain is in the Piedmont, too. It's a very large piece of granite that sticks out of the ground. It's the largest piece of granite you can see in the world!

Granite is an igneous rock. It's made of minerals like quartz, feldspar, and mica. You can see the different minerals when you hold a piece of granite in your hand. Most of the granite in America comes from Elberton! People **mine** granite here. They dig it out of the ground. The granite is mined in a **quarry**. A quarry is a place where stones are cut and moved. Granite is used for building because it's very strong! It's used for countertops, too. Georgia's granite ends up in homes all over the country!

Granite

Tires

Paint

Paste for
Wall Boards

Mica breaks in sheets, like fish scales!

Remarkable Mica

The Piedmont has some amazing minerals, like mica. Mica is found in all three types of rocks. Mica is a thin mineral. It's interesting because it breaks in sheets. The sheets look a lot like fish scales! Black mica is called biotite. Clear and white mica are called muscovite. Sand from the beach has shiny bits in it. The shiny bits are pieces of mica. Mica makes sand, soil, and rocks sparkle. Light hits mica's flat surface and makes it shine!

Mica is used in building houses. It's used in paste that makes wall boards smooth. It's used in making paint. It's also used to make tires for cars.

Biotite   Muscovite

Gneiss

Railroad Tracks

Gneiss is used in making roads.

Gneiss has stripes, like a zebra!

Gneiss is Nice!

Another neat rock in the Piedmont is called gneiss. It's pronounced like the word "nice." Gneiss is a metamorphic rock. This means it has been changed in some way. Gneiss is made when an igneous or sedimentary rock is heated or squeezed underground. This causes the rock to melt and change into gneiss. It takes a long time and a lot of heat to change a rock from one type to another!

Gneiss is used like granite. It is also very strong. You may have seen gneiss used for kitchen countertops. It's used on roadways and railroad tracks, too. You can tell if a rock is gneiss if it's made up of black and white colored bands. It's like the zebra of the rock world!

Quartz helps clocks and
watches keep time.

Quartz

Sandpaper

Quartz is used
to make jewelry.

Quartz can be pink.

Beautiful Quartz

Quartz is a mineral that is very hard and usually clear. Quartz sometimes looks like glass or diamond. It can be purple, pink, and even blue! Remember granite? Quartz is a mineral found in the rock called granite. People find lots of quartz near LaGrange.

Quartz is a very useful mineral. Can you see a clock from where you are? Do you have a watch? Quartz helps some clocks and watches keep time. Crushed quartz is used in paints and sandpaper. Amethyst, a kind of quartz, is used to make jewelry. It's a **gemstone**. A gemstone is a mineral that is used to make jewelry. There is a lot of amethyst near Tignall, Georgia.

Amethyst is a purple quartz.

Spark
Plug

Grinding
Wheel

Kyanite is
used on space
shuttles!

Bathroom
Sink

Kyanite

People once mined kyanite at Graves Mountain.

Cool Kyanite

Kyanite is a mineral found in the Piedmont. It's a blue mineral that's found in metamorphic rocks. People once mined kyanite at Graves Mountain near Lincolnton. Most of the kyanite in America once came from here! Kyanite keeps things from getting too hot. It's used in places where there is a lot of heat. It's used in making spark plugs for cars. It's used in wheels that cut and grind hard things. It's also used in making sinks and tiles for bathrooms and kitchens. Its blue color makes pretty jewelry, too.

Kyanite does a super important job for astronauts. Georgia kyanite has been used on space shuttles! It keeps important parts of the space shuttle cool when it heats up. It keeps parts of the space shuttle warm when it gets cold in space.

Garnet is used to
make jewelry.

Garnet

Garnet paper makes furniture shiny.

Good Golly Garnet!

Garnet is a mineral found in metamorphic rocks in the Piedmont. Garnets are usually red, but they can come in many different colors. There are pink garnets and yellow garnets. There are green and purple garnets! Garnets are mostly used as a gemstone. They are very shiny when polished. Garnet is also used in a type of sandpaper called garnet paper, just like quartz. Woodworkers use garnet paper to polish wood and make it smooth and shiny.

Garnets are formed deep in the earth's **crust**. This is the outer layer of the earth. It can be 30 miles deep! **Geologists** look at garnets to learn about the crust. Geologists are scientists who study rocks and minerals.

Garnets come in many colors.

Pyrite

Pyrite is sometimes used in making paper.

The Tricky Mineral, Pyrite

Pyrite is a gold-colored mineral found in the Piedmont. It's also called *fool's gold*. It looks like gold, but it's not! Pyrite is very shiny. You can see your reflection in it when it's polished. Some Native Americans used pyrite as a mirror! Today, pyrite is sometimes used in making paper. It was once mined near Hiram, Douglasville, and Villa Rica. Old mines have made holes in the ground near Marietta!

Pyrite is found in all three types of rocks. Pyrite is sometimes shaped like an ice cube. Some cubes are tiny. You would have to look at them under a magnifying glass. Some cubes can be very large, as big as a baseball. The next time you visit the Piedmont, look around. Maybe you can spot some *fool's gold*!

Pyrite is sometimes shaped like an ice cube.

Glossary

crust – The outer layer of the earth.

erosion – The process of breaking rock into sediment.

gemstone – A mineral that is used to make jewelry.

geographic region – An area named for the way the land is formed.

geologists – Scientists who study rocks and minerals.

igneous – Rocks that are made from magma.

magma – Hot liquid rock.

metal – A substance that conducts heat or electricity.

metamorphic – Rocks made when igneous or sedimentary rocks are pushed underground and heat up.

mine – To dig up a rock or a mineral from underground.

mineral – A natural material that is not alive like plants and animals.

quarry – A place where stones are cut and moved.

rock – A material that is made of two or more minerals.

rock cycle – The process by which rocks change from one type to another.

sediment – Tiny pieces of rocks broken up by rain and wind.

sedimentary – Rocks that are made from igneous rocks.

Word Index

Image Credits

p. 4   Igneous rock: © River North Photography, iStockphotography.com; Sediment: © iEverest, iStockphotography.com; Sedimentary
        rock: © Stephen Morris, iStockphotography.com; Metamorphic rock: © Gene Krebs, iStockphotography.com; Magma: © Thuerig
        Manfred, iStockphotography.com
p. 6   Piedmont hills, river: Photos courtesy of Georgia Department of Economic Development
p. 7   Clay soil: © Birgitte Magnus, iStockphotography.com
p. 8   Stone Mountain: Photo courtesy of Georgia Department of Economic Development; Countertop: © David H. Lewis,
        iStockphotography.com; Mica sample: © Melissa Carroll, iStockphotography.com; Quartz sample: © Francisco Romero,
        iStockphotography.com; Feldspar sample: © Yury Kosourov, iStockphotography.com
p. 9   Granite sample: © Sylwia Rak, iStockphotography.com
p. 10   Mica sample: © Tyler Boyes, iStockphotography.com; Tires: © Tomasz Pietryszek, iStockphotography.com; Paint: © Alistair Cotton,
        iStockphotography.com; Pasting: © Christina Richards, iStockphotography.com
p. 11   Biotite sample: © Panagiotis Milonis, iStockphotography.com; Muscovite sample: © Only Fabrizio, iStockphotography.com
p. 12   Gneiss close-up and gneiss rock: © David Woods, iStockphotography.com; Railroad tracks: © Marcus Lindstrom,
        iStockphotography.com; Paving: © Pietro Anonni, iStockphotography.com
p. 14   Pink quartz: © Manuel Velasco, iStockphotography.com; Ring: © Michael Czosnek, iStockphotography.com; Watch mechanism:
        © James Benet, iStockphotography.com; Sandpaper: © Gordon Dixon, iStockphotography.com
p. 15   Amethyst: © Stuart Pitkin, iStockphotography.com
p. 16   Graves Mountain: Photo courtesy of Georgia Department of Economic Development; Spark plug: © Edfuentesg,
        iStockphotography.com; Grinding wheel: © Ton Vols, iStockphotography.com; Space shuttle: © George Cairns,
        iStockphotography.com; Sink: © Kim Gunkel, iStockphotography.com; Kyanite sample: © Sergey Lavrenvev, iStockphotography.com
p. 18   Sanding: © Jiri Patava, fotolia.com; Ring: © Red TC, fotolia.com; Red garnet sample: © Edith Ochs, fotolia.com; Green garnet
        sample: © Alexander Maksimov, fotolia.com
p. 19   Garnet samples: © Edith Ochs, fotolia.com
p. 20   Paper: © Joakim Leroy, iStockphotography.com; Pyrite sample: © Golden Angel, fotolia.com
p. 21   Pyrite sample: © Luca Francesco Giovanni Bertolli, iStockphotography.com

Editorial Credit

Designer: Michael Sellner, Corporate Graphics, North Mankato, Minnesota

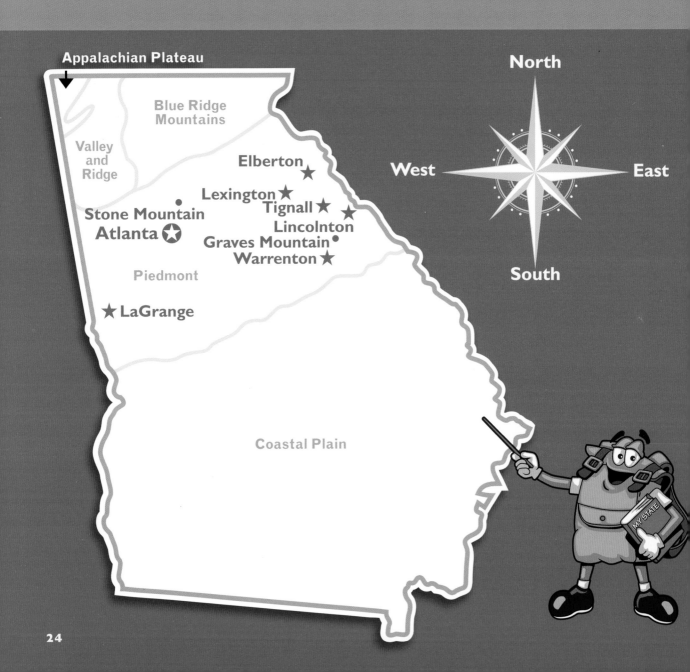

Appalachian Plateau

Blue Ridge Mountains

Valley and Ridge

Elberton

Lexington

Tignall

Stone Mountain

Lincolnton

Atlanta

Graves Mountain

Warrenton

Piedmont

LaGrange

Coastal Plain

North

West

East

South